HAVE THE ATTITUDE!

The Thinking That Makes Great Things Happen

CAROL QUINN

FOREWARD WRITTEN BY LEE COCKERELL

Former executive vice president of Disney World
and bestselling author

To James!

Carol Quinn

Have The Attitude!

The Thinking That Makes Great Things Happen

Second Edition

Copyright © 2004, 2019 by Carol Quinn

ISBN #978-0-9905876-1-3 (Soft cover)

ISBN # 978-0-9720872-3-0 (Hard cover)

ISBN # 978-0-9720872-6-1 (E-book)

Editor: Diane Sears, DiVerse Media

www.di-verse-media.com

Layout & Design: Gene Quinn

Published by HA Books

11682 Briarwood Circle, Suite 1

Boynton Beach, FL 33437

To Order Bulk Quantities – Call: 561-231-0313

SPECIAL TRIBUTE

One person, single-handedly, made this book possible. This person helped me awaken my attitude which was screaming from within to be known. Without his caring guidance, his unending wisdom and his gracious willingness to share both with me, I would have never elevated my own attitude and garnered the understanding necessary to write *Have The Attitude*. I am a living testament that it can be done and that it is good to do.

This book is dedicated in loving memory to Don McArt who was my Attitude Mentor for seven great years. No one prior, and no one since, has so profoundly and positively impacted my life. I am eternally grateful. You live on in me. I miss you.

Table of Contents

FOREWARD

Written by Lee Cockerell

T he first sentence in my book *Creating Magic: Ten Common Sense Leadership Strategies from a Life at Disney* is: "It's not magic that makes it work, it's the way we work that makes it magic." Carol Quinn's new book, *Have The Attitude: The Thinking that Makes Great Things Happen* will teach you the number one ingredient for creating magic in your life and career. I have long known that two things were responsible for my career achievements, even without a college degree: one, I have an enormous can-do positive ATTITUDE; and two, I am highly disciplined. ATTITUDE is the yeast that will enable your career to rise. Much research has been done that shows the key to success in life is ATTITUDE. You may have heard the old saying, "Good ATTITUDE, good results, bad ATTITUDE, bad results." This happens to be 100% true.

Another thing I have come to realize is that our brains lie to us. There is a bunch of negative material sitting up in that three inches above your eyes. I believe that a large percentage of what you think is not even true. Many of your thoughts, especially the subconscious ones, were put there when you were very young through different experiences like abuse, bullying, parents' behavior, society's attitude toward you, poverty, the culture and environment you grew up in, and on and on. Your ATTITUDE is a direct correlation to what is sitting up in your brain. You can begin to change this now … and this book will help you!

This book nails the power of attitude in an easy-to-understand way. It offers guidance and remedies for fixing your way of thinking. As I read it, it was like my own life flashing before me. I moved over time from a low-self-confidence person to one with more self-confidence than I could ever imagine. The number one thing that holds people back from a good or even a great life is themselves. I was not a good student, my family was very poor, my mother was married five times, I have been adopted twice, and I flunked out of college and just went to work after the Army as an entry-level employee in the hospitality business. Thirty-two years later, I was the senior operations executive for the Walt Disney World® Resort, leading 5,000 leaders and 40,000 cast members. The main thing that got me there was ATTITUDE. If you think you can, you're right. If you think you can't, you're right.

I have worked with Carol Quinn for years to understand how to select the right people — the people with the right ATTITUDE and passion. Her work has helped me tremendously in all parts of my life as it will yours. This book is a very easy read and will immediately impact the way you think. When you think differently, you do differently; and when you do differently, life just gets better and better. You can apply this to the workplace and watch your organization's results get better and better, too.

Stop thinking the way you thought in the past. You're not there anymore. As Snow Queen Elsa learned in the movie *Frozen*, you have to let it go, move forward and liberate your ATTITUDE. So LET IT GO and live to your full potential!

Lee Cockerell, Executive Vice President (Retired and Inspired), Walt Disney World® Resort, is the bestselling author of Creating Magic: Ten Common Sense Leadership Strategies From a Life at Disney, The Customer Rules: The 39 Essential Rules for Delivering Sensational Service, Time Management Magic: How to Get More Done Every Day and Move From Surviving to Thriving, and Career Magic: How to Stay on Track to Achieve a Stellar Career, and he hosts the Disney Creating Magic weekly podcast. www.LeeCockerell.com

INTRODUCTION

I wasn't even supposed to be there — it was just a total fluke. But there I was, getting out of my car at the mall shortly before noon on a weekday. I happened to look up into the sky, and at that very moment I witnessed the midair collision of two private airplanes. Four people died in that accident. I had trouble stopping myself from thinking about what I had seen.

It was a few nights later when I had the dream. There was a group of people standing around an oval asphalt track. It looked like a track behind a high school where student athletes run, but this one was at a flight school and I was an instructor.

This particular flight school was different. It taught people how to fly without using an aircraft of any kind. The students were learning how to soar like birds. After some classroom instruction, everyone would go outside to this track. They would practice their takeoffs by running around the track until they reached a speed in which their feet would lift off the ground. It was so amazing and so profoundly inspirational to see.

As with any type of training, some people got the hang of it more quickly while others were slower to catch on — not that it really mattered either way. Some, however, became frustrated and wanted to quit, and still others thought it wasn't even possible to do in the first place. As feet began to lift off the ground and people started to fly, a shift in thinking regarding what truly is possible took place. Skepticism turned to amazement. It was a phenomenal experience to witness this transformation in human potential!

You know, those four people who died in that plane crash were all pilots whose passion was flying. They lived their passion. One was a seasoned stunt pilot and the other three were Lear Jet pilots. So many of us never fulfill our dreams or accomplish our goals because we're focused on the possibility of "what if" a bad outcome were to happen.

Sure, sometimes bad things happen, and something bad happened that day. But so did something good. Those pilots never knew the lesson they had taught me. This lesson came from people I never even met. As horrible as the accident was, it showed me the brilliance of life. The chance that something bad may happen isn't enough to discourage high achievers. They take flight anyway in pursuit of their aspirations. These high fliers prefer to live life to their full potential rather than sit on the sidelines and make excuses for why they don't.

You see, all high achievers share a common thread. It just happens to be their attitude. You've heard the sayings "Attitude is everything," "Hire the attitude and teach the skill" and "It's 90 percent attitude and 10 percent skill." This is the attitude that everyone's talking about, the one that belongs to high achievers. And it's the reason these people are able to achieve better results and why they outperform most everyone else.

What exactly is their secret to success, you ask? Well, it's no longer a secret. It's has been discovered. Do you wonder whether you share this common thread with them? Do you know whether you have "The Attitude"? Can we get it if we don't already have it? Is it something that we can learn?

Your attitude, not your aptitude, will determine your altitude.

Zig Ziglar

Absolutely, yes we can have the same attitude as high achievers. Everyone can learn what the top performers have already learned, and the answers are in the pages ahead.

Perhaps it wasn't a fluke that I was in that mall parking lot that day after all, because there began the vision for flight school for the mind. Its mission, to act as a catalyst to help remove the mental barriers and reveal every person's own unlimited potential to soar to new heights, became the purpose of this book. The gift of inspiration touched me deeply that day and has never left me. That day I became an **Attitude Revolutionist** — *one who revolts against the status quo attitude and is willing to actually do something about it.* I not only practice the power of attitude for myself, I have become a passionate advocate for helping others to transform their own attitude as well as shift the attitude in the workplace.

1. WHAT DOES THE FUTURE HOLD?

E ver since the beginning of humanity, people have been fascinated with the future. To have a better sense of what lies ahead, they've come up with some very imaginative ways of trying to get more information in order to predict the future. One such way is the practice of baking small strips of paper with written predictions into a mixture of flour, sugar and oil. You probably guessed it — the fortune cookie. Randomly crack one open to learn what's in store for you. Fortune tellers, on the other hand, use crystal balls to tap into the spiritual world and look at the palms of people's hands to foresee their future. Then there's the daily horoscope, a forecast of a person's future based on the positions of the stars and planets at the time they were born. And of course, there this one: watching the sky and tracking the formation of clouds, also known as weather forecasting.

Here's what has been predicted for me today:

> **DAILY HOROSCOPE** – Mental and emotional confusion rule your day today. Your best course of action may be to fall silent.

> **TODAY'S WEATHER FORECAST** – Overcast, gloomy with 80% chance of rain. May as well cancel your plans.

> **ECONOMIC OUTLOOK** – The economy is heading toward a recession with little chance for recovery anytime soon.

Sounds like there's good reason to feel depressed, right? Some of us may not even want to get out of bed. But how can people be so sure about how things are going to turn out? Unlike the past, the future — be it five years, five days, or five minutes from now — hasn't happened yet. Those million-to-one odds of winning the lottery pay off to someone almost every week. Things that "will never happen in a million years," happen and "sure things" often don't. Whatever is going to happen is really anyone's guess.

Predicting the future is something everyone does every day, whether we realize it or not. Predictions about what's likely to happen vary among people. They can differ only slightly or be polar-opposites — like night and day. Everyone has the freedom to believe what they want when it comes to the future. People can choose to be positive and upbeat about what's to come or they can choose to be downtrodden and sad. Not knowing the future really frightens many of us. We conjure up the worst-case scenario then become paralyzed with fear. According to Abraham Lincoln, the 16th president of the United States, "The best way to predict your future is to create it." A person can only say that when he knows the future is indeed ours to create.

2. WHERE GREAT ACCOMPLISHMENTS BEGIN

I f you were to list mankind's greatest accomplishments, what would you include? Would you include putting man on the moon, building a reusable spacecraft, or the invention of the airplane? How about the discovery of anesthesia, antibiotics, X-rays, or the cure for many illnesses and diseases? Or all those conveniences we take for granted such as electricity, televisions, microwave ovens, computers and cell phones? What about the Pyramids in Egypt, the Great Wall of China and the Golden Gate Bridge, just to mention a few of the greatest architectural wonders of the world? Did you know that the Golden Gate Bridge was thought to be impossible to construct at one time? Then there is the Stealth Bomber, a plane that's nearly invisible to enemies. Advancements in technology seem to have no end in sight.

All accomplishments have a starting point. A beginning. And this beginning is the same no matter what success is achieved in the end. Just like everything on the list above, before a man could land on the moon, it had to be thought to be possible — before it actually was. For this project to even begin, someone had to believe this monumental task could be achieved. At least one person had to believe it was within reach. I am sure there were plenty of skeptics who thought the undertaking was "pie in the sky." They were the ones pointing out all the reasons why it would never work. As the successes accumulated, however, I'm guessing these cynics had a change of mind. They got on board and believed after they saw it happen. One mindset needs to see it to believe it and the other believes it to see it.

The one thing all great accomplishments have in common is that they began with a thought or idea that it could indeed be accomplished. This thought was focused in the light of possibility — not in the darkness of inevitable defeat. Obstacles, failures, roadblocks and setbacks were all a part of changing the impossible to the possible ... they always are. But for those willing to believe, these impediments to success aren't enough to deter their optimism about what can be.

13

3. PROVING YOURSELF RIGHT

Working diligently to figure out a way to transform the impossible into being possible is how optimists prove their thinking right. Working relentlessly to find a way to achieve something people deem impossible would prove their negative, pessimistic viewpoint is wrong. And if you've ever noticed, people don't work too hard to prove that their own thinking is incorrect. It's the people who believe something can be done who are doing the hard work to find a solution. They're willing to work overtime on their own dime if that's what it takes. It's more than just coincidence — it's physiology. They just can't help it. That's because all of us are wired to prove ourselves right. Ponder the magnitude of that!!

As human beings, we have a thinking process that is hardwired to bring about whatever we believe is true. Said another way, we

14

work to manifest our thoughts and beliefs. It's this design that links our behaviors, our responses, our actions and lack of, to our thoughts. Our actions aren't random or without rhyme or reason but rather are directly linked and in response to our thoughts.

This hardwiring that exists within everyone works the same way whether you believe you can achieve something or believe you cannot. It can work in your favor to help you achieve a goal or it can hold you back from doing your best. Which way matters not to the hardwiring. It works in either direction just fine. It also works whether you are aware of it or not. It simply follows orders without questioning them.

An easy way to understand how the power of thought operates is to compare high achievers with those who achieve less. The difference is simple. High achievers have figured out how to use this power to their advantage. They have learned about the payoff that exists when you see things from an optimistic viewpoint, an outlook that's in alignment with success. This type of thinking pays off in their favor with the creation of more desirable outcomes.

When Cesar Chavez was organizing the United Farm Workers of America, he challenged union members to say, "Si, se puede" when they didn't know how they would overcome obstacles. It means, "Yes, we can do it" or "Yes, it is possible." The farmworkers didn't

15

think they could win without violence, but Chavez believed differently. Like Hindu leader Mahatma Gandhi, Chavez believed a mission could be accomplished through persistence, hard work and faith. He believed the farmworkers could advance economic and social conditions through non-violent means, and that's exactly what they did.

Even when high achievers don't know how to achieve a goal, they still believe it's possible. They have an almost unrealistic knowingness that believes in a good outcome without having any evidence to back it up. They first conceive possibility, that it can be done, and then automatically follow these thoughts with thoughts focused on figuring out how. Then that is followed by the necessary action and effort until they achieve the goal. It's all just an automatic process to prove their optimistic thinking is right that is working *in their favor*. You get the thinking right and the action automatically follows.

It's nothing magical. It's not even luck. It's just using the power of thought to one's advantage.

It's also working the exact same way for those who achieve less, except here the power of thought is being used to work against them.

From the start, they think a particular outcome is unlikely or that it's impossible. This is believed to be true. Since they are unable to conceptualize it, they can't see what they need to do in order to make it happen. Just like optimists, pessimists will also produce the appropriate response for their thinking. This time, however, the response will work to prove it can't be done. They are less engaged, and less effort is put forth, ultimately confirming they were correct — they couldn't achieve the goal.

It's not that optimism is more powerful and pessimism is less powerful. They have equal potency to create. It's that optimism is more powerful at creating good outcomes and desirable results, and it's what enables us to take flight. The power of thought can be used just as easily to sabotage a person's own success as it can to advance it. Caring more about the thoughts we think is in our own best interest. For many, *what you think* just became more important than we ever had imagined.

4. THE WAY WE THINK

I n an interview with a magazine, I was asked about the role of optimism and pessimism in job performance, and how it shows up differently during the interview and hiring process. The woman interviewing me for this article asked skeptically, "Do you mean to tell me that people really say they can't or couldn't do something regarding their job and then blame others for the reason why?" She added, "Wouldn't they know better than to say something like that?" I replied by telling her that's exactly what happens, and it happens a lot. That's because people actually believe it when they say there was nothing they could do. And that's why they say it. A note for interviewers and hiring managers: The trick to exposing this information lies in using motivation-based interviewing and in the way you phrase your interview questions. It's not hard at all once you learn this.

How we think and how we analyze information is a process we began learning early in childhood. The experts say a child's brain is 80 percent developed by age 7. Multiple factors influence the cognitive development of thinking and reasoning. This period in childhood is called the "formative years." Over time, this newly formed thinking process takes hold and becomes the only way that person knows how to think. By adulthood it's so entrenched it's an unconscious reflex or a habit. This routine way of thinking becomes a person's attitude.

Google's online dictionary defines *attitude* as a settled way of thinking that is typically reflected in a person's behavior. Some synonyms for attitude are: way of looking at things, school of thought, mindset, outlook, perspective, slant, and how one reacts. This book defines attitude as *one's tendency to think and behave in either a positive or a negative manner.* Tendency, being a key word, means a person's inclination toward a particular way of thinking and behaving. A person's attitude becomes most evident as a tendency in the face of challenge.

Attitude is our mental outlook regarding what we expect will happen. It's our positive and negative predictions. It's this preference toward one way of thinking or the other that's labeled an "I can" attitude or "I can't" attitude. And our attitude drives everything! The words we speak. What we do and don't do. And what we will and won't accomplish will ultimately be driven by the attitude we have.

Many adults lose objectivity when it comes to their own attitude, simply insisting their way of seeing things is normal and right. Unaware of the mechanics of thought, they keep thinking the way they always have regardless of their results.

The thinking process is often not viewed as something that's more effective or less effective. Perhaps since we really cannot remember a time when we didn't know how to think, we believe we were born knowing how and just assume we're doing it well. It's not as if we see our own thinking as being wrong or defective. If we did, we wouldn't think it. Too often we see everyone else as being the problem ... not us or our thinking.

Since how we think is a learned process, have you ever stopped to consider that perhaps not everyone learned how to do it in an effective way? Or that one way of thinking can produce completely different results than another way of thinking, with some results being better than others? In our fast-paced lives, I don't believe most people have stopped and given serious consideration to the idea that it's our thinking that's really behind our successes and failures.

5. TWO TYPES OF THINKING

T he more you have the opportunity to observe various job performance levels, the more you are able to see that a person's thinking process has the single greatest impact on what that person accomplishes. It ultimately explains why some people achieve more while others often struggle just to achieve very little.

How a person thinks about the future and what's likely to happen falls into two groups or types of thought even though the thoughts themselves are infinite.

The first group is made up of those thoughts that are action-oriented. They are those thoughts that envision a positive or desirable outcome as one that is possible. They are focused on how to accomplish the desired outcome, and as a result, they generate the necessary action to achieve the envisioned outcome. They are not only solution-oriented, they put a person in motion to create that outcome. They genuinely support the belief that the best can happen. These thoughts are part of the "I can" attitude, also known in this book as THE ATTITUDE.

The second group, made up of passive thoughts, belongs to the prophets of doom. Passive thoughts predict future outcomes as being negative or contrary to the desired outcome. They come from the belief that a specific outcome cannot be achieved and should be labeled as unrealistic. These thoughts are passive because they discourage action and effort with their "Why bother to try? There is nothing I can do about it" perspective. They constrict thinking, discard options and close off the mind to solutions. As a result, they produce very different outcomes than the first group. This kind of attitude tends to never take flight, but if it does, it doesn't remain in flight.

Positive thought focuses on possibility and expands the mind in search of a solution. Additionally, more solutions appear to those who are open to their existence and are seeking them out. It's not as if only positive thoughts work and negative ones don't. Realize that both types of thought are equally powerful. They both work perfectly to create the outcome that's equivalent to the thinking.

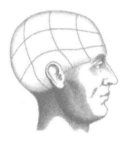

6. CONTROL: WHERE DOES IT RESIDE?

T he amount of control people believe they have to impact their lives and their outcomes has its own specialized area of study within psychology called "locus of control." According to psychologist Hebert Lefcourt, in his book titled *Locus of Control,* "Whether people believe that they can determine their own fate, within limits, is of critical importance to the way in which they engage in challenges." Control boils down to how much power a person believes he or she has to produce intended results by conquering the obstacles that block the way.

Locus of control is a self-efficacy psychology and it's about how effective or ineffective a person is at producing the desired outcomes. The word locus means location. Locus of control is the location where power or control over future results is thought to reside. In other words, it's who or what gets to determine an outcome. It is either believed to be internal, meaning the power is within oneself to achieve a goal, or it is not, in which case control is seen as being external of oneself. The latter implies that one's actions will not impact what happens. The words "power" and "control" are used interchangeably because who or what has power also has control.

An external source of power could be anyone or anything other than oneself — who or what isn't important. It doesn't matter whether the external controller is specifically identified, such as "the boss," or it's more ambiguous, such as "they" or bad luck, destiny or fate. What's important is it's believed to be not oneself.

What we think we *can* and *can't* control varies among people. For example, most of us would agree that we cannot control the weather, so we don't even try. But not 100 percent will agree with this. Some people believe that we do have some control over our weather and we could have more control if we figured out how. For example, Native Americans have long used rain dance rituals to cause precipitation, and modern researchers have studied ways to alter weather through the science of cloud seeding.

What one person believes is impossible, another person thinks is attainable. It goes back to the beginning of the book about our prediction of an outcome. You see, in order to give ourselves the go-ahead to try, we must think that it's possible to achieve before we'll expend the necessary effort to make it happen. There may be nothing more powerful than a made-up mind.

This makes location of control tied to motivation. An internal locus of control is also known as internally or intrinsically motivated as well as "self-motivated." It's what makes you see yourself as possessing the power to affect an outcome or, more specifically, to achieve the desired outcome. You are the driver, you put yourself into motion and you steer yourself to the desired outcome. You know it's likely you will get there as long as you don't quit trying. You are determined and persist as a result of your thinking.

External control, on the other hand, means you see yourself as being powerless to affect, control or determine an outcome. People who do not believe in their own power see the external world as being in charge. They see themselves at a disadvantage, as merely being passengers who have little say in their own destinations.

Locus of control is a learned thought process, and the difference between an internal and external perception of control is just a variance in thinking, that's all. It's a perception. It's not that some people have power to create and others don't. It's a point of view only, but it's so powerful that it determines what people create. The perspective that the external world is in charge and there's nothing a person can do is a view that sees oneself as being insignificant or inconsequential — meaning to have no influence. This misconception is nothing more than a learned way of thinking that distorts reality in a way that makes it harder for the person to achieve goals.

All people have more control to affect outcomes than they realize. The key is to become more aware of the thoughts that see us as lacking power and then replace them with truer thoughts, ones that recognize our own power. It sounds simple enough ... right?

When perceived control is not recognized, it's believed to not even exist at all. The person's negative thinking conceals the truth about his or her actual power and potential. It sabotages their success by rendering them powerless in their own eyes. To them, it really is the external world that's doing them wrong, not their own thinking. They cannot see it any other way ... at least at the moment.

In any situation or experience in which people see themselves as being helpless to create a better outcome, they have given their power away to someone or something else to create it for them. Sadly, they become more vulnerable to outcomes they don't want. This means a person's perception of control plays a critical component in achievement and success. Locus of control — it's a perception that very much matters.

26

7. OBSTACLES VERSUS ATTITUDE

T he development or underdevelopment of people's locus of control makes all the difference in the world in how they view the obstacles that block their path to a goal. Let's use the analogy of a balance scale to explain how obstacles are viewed differently between internally and externally motivated people. This particular type of scale has a T-shaped frame and two pans, one connected to each side. It is used to compare the weight of two different items when one is placed in each pan.

Imagine that we place the amount of power we see ourselves having to conquer obstacles and affect outcomes (aka our attitude) in the left pan. On the other side of the scale, the right pan, let's place the obstacle, adversity or whatever blocks our path to achieving the desired outcome. This pan would have uncooperative people, difficult problems, not enough time, lack of money or resources, unfortunate circumstances, illness or whatever roadblocks you are up against.

This scale does not measure in pounds and ounces or grams like most scales. Instead, it compares the two sides to each other to determine which weighs more. This scale uses our own judgment to assess what each side is believed to weigh.

Here is how it works: Whichever side is believed to have the most power and control over an outcome weighs the most. In reality, however, only the left side of the scale that contains our attitude matters. It's this side that will ultimately determine who or what has control over the outcome. I'll explain why.

The actual size of the difficulty on the right side of the scale is almost irrelevant. That may seem odd at first but here's why it's so. If the person making the assessment does not realize his own power, meaning he underestimates himself and what he can do, the obstacle will almost always appear to weigh more than his side of the scale does. When a person underestimates his own power to conquer obstacles, then everything is skewed. Both sides of the scale are viewed incorrectly. When we see ourselves as small and inconsequential, from that vantage point the rest of the world looks much larger than it really is. It could be compared to a child's view of the world, where adults all appear to be giant-like and in charge. It boils down to the size of a person's attitude toward conquering obstacles. It's the most important measurement of all.

Underestimating what we can achieve is more common than you may think. It's almost an epidemic problem. When we underestimate ourselves, this perspective causes us to believe expending effort is futile. Obstacles appear insurmountable. But seeing them as being larger than us is not an issue of having a problem that's truly insurmountable or impossible to conquer. The real issue is the undersized attitude, and attitude is nothing more than a point of view.

The view of obstacles will change inversely as the size of the attitude changes. As the attitude grows larger, obstacles appear smaller. If the attitude shrinks, those same obstacles seem gigantic. The size of the obstacle never actually changed. Said another way, the T-scale only tips in one direction or the other when the attitude changes and is not altered by the size of the obstacle.

8. SHEDDING RESPONSIBILITY

T he "I can't," "It can't be done" or any similar beliefs must be justified or proved right just as all thinking must be. People use supporting data, viewpoints, facts and whatever else they can put their hands on to build their case. It's known as *confirmation bias* and it's when we use only information that favors our existing point of view. Everything that does not support it is left out. Here, thought, time and energy are being spent going in the direction of their thinking but going in the opposite direction from the goal. We really can justify just about anything in our own minds if we try.

Take the time to listen to what other people say. Negative, "I can't" comments will involve the relinquishing of personal responsibility, or the shifting of power off of and away from that person and onto someone or something else. You might hear, "I can't do it *because...*" or "It can't be done *because...*" and this explanation will reveal that person's external placement of power. "I don't have my homework because the dog ate it." It's the dog's fault! This power shifting is the always-present counterpart to "I can't" thinking and an easy giveaway to an under-developed sense of power. In the workplace, it's a common behavior of the disengaged. You may even want to pay closer attention and listen to what you're really saying. Not only can you hear other people's attitude, others can hear yours.

This shifting or relinquishing of power screams out the message, "I see myself as the weaker one at the mercy of the external world!" Oblivious to the sabotage their own thinking is doing to themselves, "I can't" thinkers believe they are held back by external forces. If a person sees himself as a victim in a situation, or is playing the victim, then he also thinks no one could consider him responsible for the outcome that happens. His logic is simple. He is thinking, "Just explain that something or someone else was in complete charge and that takes me off the hook, and everyone should understand this the way that I do."

Thinking that relinquishes one's own power to affect an outcome stops the learning process from taking place. Being a poor performer isn't always a bad thing. Every high performer performs poorly in the beginning. It's not learning and growing that's the real problem. For those who remain poor performers, asking themselves, "What could I have learned from this and what can I do differently next time?" goes against the "There's nothing I could have done about it" mindset. Altering this story would invalidate their "I'm powerless" explanation, so they stick with it. The cycle then repeats all over again because nothing was learned.

A good example of this is when a person keeps changing jobs because of a terrible boss. It's the boss who didn't understand that the job demands were unrealistic or that the customers were impossible to please. The next boss treats this person unjustly, too. It's one misunderstanding after another, but it's never this person's fault. The bosses were the problem. This person has a "Why always me?" sentiment. I remember a story about a low-performing teacher who eventually was released from his job. He responded by saying, "I could have been a better teacher if only I'd had better students."

The tremendous damage of shifting control to an external source is that it belittles the people shifting the control and conceals their power from themselves, resulting in a continuation of the belief in powerlessness.

We are the ones doing the damage to ourselves and we can't even see it. There may be some instant relief when we take responsibility off ourselves, but the long-term damage to "self" often goes unrecognized because the blame is continually placed elsewhere. As long as we are steadfast in our thinking and our thinking remains limited, so will our results. Interestingly, theoretical physicist and author Stephen Hawking noted that "...even people who claim everything is predestined, and that we can do nothing to change it, look before they cross the road." Things aren't as predestined and beyond our control as we may think.

9. CHOICES CHOICES CHOICES

U nfortunately, many of us grew up without learning about our power or how to operate it in a way that serves us well. If we never learn to manage our thoughts, our thoughts can run out of control and manage us instead. It's not something that happens on purpose. It's more like an unruly child who never learned the difference between appropriate and inappropriate behavior and is being allowed to do whatever he wants. It's not the child's fault. But as this child grows up, his poor choices in behavior create a lot of problems for him and others.

As adults, however, we are responsible for the results our thinking and our actions create. Being problem-focused comes from never learning a better way, but we're still responsible for the results, or lack of, that it creates.

34

I remember a fictional story of a man trapped in a cellar for many years. This man would scream out, "Let me out! Let me out!" He would shout for help, but no one ever came to his rescue. He would kick and beat on the door, but it never opened. One day he became so fed up with his situation that he decided once and for all to find a way to get out. He went to the door and began jiggling the doorknob, and amazingly the door sprang open. To his surprise, he discovered the door had never been locked. In fact, it had no lock at all. The man had assumed he was trapped against his will when he was the one who had held the key to his own freedom all along but had never realized it.

Comprehending that you have choices and control over what you think is the foundation for more effective thinking. It's one of the secrets of high achievement.

At any given time, we have much more control to create our outcomes than we recognize or accept. Think about it. Every day, in every moment, we have control over our many choices. We can speak up kindly or harshly, or we can say nothing at all. We can ask for assistance or assume no one will help. We can choose to accept what we don't want or do something to change it. We can walk away or we can keep trying.

We can say we have no alternative, or we can see more options. We can think happy thoughts or sad ones. We can see a person's good points or we can focus only on a person's flaws. We can see the most hopeful outcome or dwell on the worst-case scenario. We can get stuck in the past or see the best that's yet to come. We can find things to be grateful for or choose resentment for what we lack. We can change our own attitude or insist others need to change.

When we get knocked down, we can get back up or we can stay down. We can help ourselves or wait to be helped. We can even turn help down when it shows up. We can give up, give in or give of ourselves. We can look for solutions and ways to make things better or choose to believe solutions do not exist.

Choices, choices, choices. We all have them, even when we don't want to admit it. At any time, we can choose a different option than we chose yesterday. Yet, too often I hear people say, "I had no choice," "My hands were tied" or "There was nothing I could do." Know the difference between not liking an option, not wanting to do one of the options … and not having any options.

Here's an example. Let's say you hate your present job. You have some options here. You can wait for the boss to see things differently and to change because the boss, after all, is the problem. You can be negative and bad-mouth your boss and the company and express how miserable you are every chance you get. You can voice how unfair you think things are and explain all the flaws you've found in the organization. You can act disinterested and do only the bare minimum you can get away with and be a disengaged, low-performing employee.

You can choose one or more of these above options, all of which probably will make you look bad, even though you feel justified in your choice of behavior.

Now, there are also more choices, ones that would benefit you more. You could put on a happy face. You may try looking for a different position within the same company or take on tasks that would make you more marketable for your next job. You could perform your job well and project a positive attitude, which instead would enhance your professional reputation. You could keep your negativity to yourself and say nothing when you can't say anything good, all at the same time you are hunting for a new job.

See the positive, say something nice, smile, show interest, go the extra mile, find a solution. Or add to the problem, show frustration and anger, be negative, become indifferent, act disengaged, make things more difficult. All of these are choices, and they are under your control. Discarding them, discrediting them, not considering them as being viable options or not recognizing them as options does not change the fact that they are still options available to you. Everything you do or don't do will have an effect.

Make a change in your thinking in either direction, from pessimistic to positive or from positive to negative, and watch how the world responds to you differently than before. If something isn't working in our lives, if we are stuck in poor results, it typically means there is a change that we need to make. We have more power to influence our experiences than most people recognize simply by seeing all the options rather than limiting them.

10. 90,000 UNITS OF ENERGY

H ere is another way to look at attitude that may help you to better understand its power and how it works. The mind is a very busy place. We think approximately 90,000 thoughts per day. However, you can think only one thought at a time. You can switch from one to another instantly but still have only one at time. While you are thinking one thought, such as "I can't," you cannot also think in the terms of possibility and work toward finding a solution. You cannot believe that you both lack power and possess it at the same time regarding the same issue.

Think of each thought as being one unit of energy with each day having about 90,000 units of energy available. Where you place your attention becomes the focus of your energy. The greater the focus, the greater the energy you give to shaping the outcome. Imagine every positive thought propelling you in the right direction. Just think what you could achieve and the altitude you could reach with a mind full of "I can" thought energy. Think of high achievers as people who spend most of their time thinking "I can" thoughts and figuring out solutions to those things they don't know how to do.

Speaking of altitude, U.S. astronaut Edgar Mitchell, the lunar module pilot aboard the Apollo 14 mission to the moon in 1971, said it boldly:

"Mass is merely dense thought."

Where you place your focus is what you create. The invention of the computer, for example, started out as an idea. It eventually grew from an intangible thought form into mass form or physical form.

Those 90,000 units of thought energy are pure power. What we often do, however, is make the mistake of giving some of our thought to the desired outcome but then giving more thought to how it probably won't happen. Or we get into trouble with thinking that only selected thoughts of ours have power and the rest do not. It doesn't work that way. We are using our power every second of every day to prove that we can or prove that we can't, or we're diluting our power by mixing it between both beliefs. We reduce our power to achieve goals when we don't use all of the power that we have available to us effectively. The thoughts we focus on the most have the single greatest impact on our life. What you choose to think about is where you are directing your power and determines the direction you will take.

In the movie *Back to the Future*, which is about time travel, an optimistic character named George McFly says, "If you put your mind to it, you can accomplish anything!" Unfortunately, there are many times when we don't make up our minds that we can achieve, so we never fully unleash the power we possess, at least not as much as we could.

Another famous optimist of film, Master Yoda from *Star Wars*, had THE ATTITUDE. He said, "Try not. Do or do not do!" That quote is about making up your mind to do something or choosing not to do it, but not doing something halfheartedly in between. It's about either finding a way to achieve or not even trying — "Try not." To say you'll *try* means you'll expend some effort and maybe you'll do what it takes to achieve results and maybe you won't. It's a mind that is not fully made up or convinced, which means it is not operating in its full power.

Some people choose to reject it because they don't want to take responsibility for the outcomes they create — especially the bad ones. Rejection of one's power doesn't actually diminish the existence of the person's power. It merely deceives the person who is in denial.

There are many who inadvertently misuse their power because they don't yet know they have it.

The power of attitude exists. And it's not about whether we're one of the chosen few who have it. It's about whether we choose to believe we have it or not. It's about how we use the power that we and everyone already have. The same power is being used whether we think we can or think we can't. Both become self-fulfilling predictions. It's only the "I can" attitude, however, that's using the power to achieve goals.

What really distinguishes people from each other is less about their physical differences or their varied personal circumstances but rather what they create with their power. *Attitude really is everything!*

11. THE PLACEBO EFFECT

H ere's a question for you to ponder. If it's really true that your thoughts have this much power and can greatly affect your results, would you choose different thoughts? It makes us stop and wonder about how responsibly or effectively we are all thinking. It also causes us to look a little differently at the role we are all playing in constructing our own results.

The power of thought is often underestimated. Take, for example, *placebo*, which means, "I shall please." The power of the placebo effect has been accepted in the medical and research communities for a long time, yet not everyone knows about it. This is how it works: To test the effectiveness of a new drug, participants in a study group are given either the actual drug or a placebo, a pill that looks just like the drug but is made of sugar. Unable to tell the difference, participants do not know which they are receiving.

In study after study, placebos work! In a 1950s study, the placebo was 70 percent as effective as morphine for controlling pain. Drug companies would have no logical reason to test their medication against placebos if placebos had no effect. But they do! The placebo's power comes from the patient's positive expectation of being helped. Expectation plays a powerful role in the placebo effect.

According to the *Oxford English Dictionary*, a placebo is a medicine or procedure prescribed for the psychological benefit to the patient rather than for any physiological effect. Despite being fake medicine, placebos have a tremendous psychological impact. That by no means suggests that the patient's pain is all in the head. It's not saying the discomfort is not real. To the contrary. According to an article in *USA Today* titled "Take one. You'll feel better," hundreds of scientists at the National Institutes of Health in Bethesda, Maryland, discussed what was known and not known about the placebo effect. They not only discussed the scientific research data, they spoke of the healing power of hope and expectation. Patients who focused on or believed there was a chance they would feel better and recover responded favorably even in the absence of the drug or placebo. Scientists speculate that a placebo works by stimulating endorphins in the brain. Ethicist Howard

Brody, a family practitioner at Michigan State University, says, "You don't need the sugar pill to unleash these important forces." The placebo effect suggests that cures do not just come from pill bottles or high-tech equipment or procedures, that engaging the power of the mind to aid in the healing process has greater potential than we have yet discovered.

It seems that thinking good thoughts not only feels good, it's also good for us. Some researchers have gone as far as to suggest that pessimism may be harmful to your health by boosting levels of destructive stress hormones in your bloodstream. No one completely understands how a positive attitude helps people recover more quickly, but mounting evidence suggests it has something to do with the mind's power.

A study in the 1960s gave 12 psychology graduate students several rats to train. Half of the students were told they were working with genetically bred rats that were very smart and would learn quickly. The other half were told their rats were genetically bred to be slow learners. At the end of the experiment, it was determined that the "smart" rats did, indeed, learn exceptionally well and that the "stupid" rats did, in fact, do poorly. However, there was one catch. What the students did not know is that there was no difference between the rats. The rodents were all the same. None of them had been genetically altered.

Similar experiments have been conducted with schoolchildren and their teachers, and also at the U.S. Air Force Academy with enlisted airmen, all which produced the same kinds of results. Some teachers were told they had a group of slow learners and others were told they were teaching gifted students. All of the students, however, were similar in their learning ability — yet the results were equivalent to what the teachers believed.

The power of your beliefs or expectations does have an effect on what happens. What you think an outcome will be in advance of it happening does affect your results. Changing your prediction, changing what you think, could in fact make all the difference in the world in the results you achieve.

As it turned out, in the study involving the rats, the students who believed they had superior rats treated their rats differently than those students who thought their rats wouldn't learn no matter what they did. It was out of their control, meaning their efforts would not produce a good outcome, *or so they thought*. Instead of handling their rats gently, giving them attention and coaxing them with treats, as the students with the so-called "smart" rats did, the students who thought they had unintelligent rats handled them very sparingly —

and when they did, they only picked them up by their tails. What they thought did affect their actions, which did have a powerful impact on what ultimately happened. Instead of the rats being the experiment, it was the students' thinking that was studied. Simply a change in thinking could have produced a different set of results for those who believed there was nothing they could do.

12. HUMAN KRYPTONITE

W hen people don't know about their power, they think they don't have it. They lack awareness of the role they're playing in creating their own outcomes and experiences. They think someone or something else is doing it to them. But that's not the only thing some people are unaware of. The word "negative" refers to something that's not good. Someone with an attitude that's not good would have no problem changing it to one that's more positive … right? Apparently, it's much easier to recognize negativity in someone else. We often are unwilling to see it in ourselves. Most people tend to place themselves into the category of being positive thinkers even when they are not. Lacking awareness of one's own negative attitude and its effects often gets people into situations they don't like and don't know how to get out of because they can't see their role in creating it.

48

Merriam Webster's Dictionary defines the word "negative" as: opposed to the positive, containing negation, having lower potential or being without reward or result, to lack constructiveness or helpfulness, arguing against a resolution, to disprove, deny or refute. It's not hard to see why negative people struggle to achieve their goals with unconstructive beliefs and behaviors that are so resistant to forward progress.

People often don't fully comprehend the extent of their own negative thinking for several reasons. One reason is because they deem their dire predictions not as being negative but rather as being "realistic." Or they don't see their venting, whining and complaining as lacking constructiveness but instead they see it as being justified. And their absence of helpful problem-solving efforts isn't "negative" either. What's negative about not trying when you can't impact an outcome after all? They not only lack awareness of their own negative attitude, they're unaware of the effect it's having on them and their results. It's this lack of awareness that keeps a person from changing and therefore stuck.

If having a positive attitude is so good for us, then why isn't everyone flocking to get one?

49

That's because acknowledging the power of attitude comes with a huge responsibility. First, we must admit we're doing something that's not working. That's hard for people who insist it's not their fault or need to be right all the time. Next, we must do the work to change our own attitude. Yes, it takes work. That's a problem for the unmotivated and the unwilling. Add to that the fact that many people have learned how to get away with behaving poorly and avoid the negative consequences of being held accountable. Since they have gotten away with it for so long, what reason do they have to change now? They simply give another convincing speech about how they'll do better — but then don't change. Or they stay on their best behavior for a while until things settle down — then go back to the way they were. Many test the limits to see what someone will and won't tolerate. Some only associate with those who are willing to put up with them. But perhaps the greatest reason people don't acknowledge the power of attitude is because of the obligation and responsibility to create better results that comes with it.

The world is full of "willing" people — those willing to do the work and those willing to let others do it.

For the latter, it's simply easier for them to believe they can't.

In my best-selling SHRM-published book titled *Motivation-Based Interviewing: A Revolutionary Approach to Hiring the Best*, a how-to book on assessing attitude and hiring high achievers, negative thoughts are compared to Kryptonite, a fictional substance that depletes Superman's energy and drains his power. Some people carry around their own kryptonite, usually without realizing it. Drained of their energy, unable to soar, they become mere mortals, capable of nothing more than average performance.

Imagine all human beings having the power to be just like Superman, to do remarkable work and soar to great heights, if they'd simply lose their negative attitude. Sadly, they spend all their energy resisting the change and transformation that would lead them to the discovery of their superpowers.

13. LIFE REFLECTS ATTITUDE

M any people think their attitude is justified based on their life. Once their life improves, their attitude will, too. But it's the other way around. Your life reflects your attitude and won't change until your attitude changes.

It really is exactly as American automobile magnate Henry Ford said: "Whether you think you can or you cannot, you're right." You are what you think you are. When it comes to achieving goals, it makes a big difference what kinds of thoughts you think. You and only you have the choice of how you envision an outcome, where you place your focus, and whether you think you can or cannot, all of which will have the greatest impact on you, the one thinking the thoughts.

The power of attitude is a lot like the making of a movie. What you think will unfold in front of your very eyes. What you think will determine your actions and your actions, or lack of, and will play a significant role in creating your results. Your actions make you the lead actor playing out the script that you wrote in your mind. Only by changing your thoughts can you change the script and the role you play. We are the script writer in the movie starring ourselves acting out what we think. As the star in your own movie, you should know the tremendous power of the "I can" attitude. It shouts "ACTION!" It says, "I have the power! I can prevail over the obstacle!" It proclaims to you, and everyone watching your movie, that you have THE ATTITUDE that makes great things happen.

Lucky for us, our attitude doesn't manifest instantly. We have time to change our thinking. That delay, however, often keeps us from connecting our current outcomes with our prior thoughts. Thoughts often don't manifest figuratively either. For example, no one ever wishes to be in a car accident, but accidents happen all the time. Thoughts like "Bad things always seem to happen to me" or "I can never get ahead" act like magnets that attract setbacks.

That doesn't mean setbacks and bad things don't happen to positive thinkers. But when they do, these people are better equipped to successfully navigate through them. Their optimistic

"Life is for me" mindset enables them to keep moving forward and even see the good in a bad situation. People who don't comprehend that they have control in their life and over their life develop a sense of passivity and helplessness, according to Bernie Siegel, a physician, speaker and bestselling author known for encouraging people to tap into their own healing power to overcome adversity. Evidence shows that your attitude about life can improve your health and even speed your recovery time from a serious illness, surgery or loss.

TV talk show host and bestselling author Iyanla Vanzant, in her book *Until Today*, states:

It is arrogant of you to assume that you are incapable because you don't believe you are capable. You have gifts. You have the gift of intellect. You can think yourself into and out of any situation with which you are confronted. You have the ability to speak for yourself. You can defend yourself! That is power. You are powerful! Now, why don't you try acting like it? Just for today, know that you are powerful. Embrace your power! Start by being grateful for the power you have been given and are using free of charge! Today I am devoted to experiencing myself as a powerful being!

Suzanne Segerstrom, Ph.D., a University of Kentucky Psychology Department assistant professor who has studied the effects of optimism on a person's health, said this about the connection between attitude and positive outcomes: "The attitude that seems to help the most is optimism, hope and, above all, a feeling that you have some control over or can have an impact on the quality of your own life."

14. ONE TRUTH

N o human being is better than or less than another human being. However, we seem to have an epidemic problem with people who think they aren't good enough. They have low self-worth and view themselves negatively. A healthy self-worth, when we feel positive about ourselves and about life in general, better equips us to deal with life's ups and downs. We feel good about ourselves whether we succeed or fail. When we see ourselves and life in a more negative light, we feel less able to take on challenges. We avoid things we find challenging by saying "I can't."

According to Chris Williams, a professor of psychosocial psychiatry at the University of Glasgow, "In the short term, avoiding challenging and difficult situations makes you feel a lot safer. In the longer term, this can backfire because it reinforces your underlying doubts and fears. It teaches you the unhelpful rule that the only way to cope is by avoiding things."

People learn how to think at an early age, and their self-worth begins to form during childhood, too.

Messages about our worth are taken in from our experiences, our environment and the people around us.

Whatever messages are absorbed often stay with us and travel into adulthood.

When children learn to value their own opinions and feel deserving of the respect of others, they have developed a healthy self-worth. They have learned the truth about themselves as human beings. When the opposite messages are taken in and children aren't validated, they tend to go in one of two directions. In some instances, they become adults who are people pleasers who place greater value on the opinions, needs and desires of other people and less value on their own. In other words, they overvalue others and undervalue themselves. These pleasers often have a tough time standing up for themselves, making them easy targets to be taken advantage of. They often see only the good in others, causing them to miss important warning signs. You could say their people filter is broken. They tend to become trapped in trying to get validation from those who will never give it to them.

In other instances, narcissistic tendencies are developed that lead to overvaluing oneself and undervaluing others. These people often control and manipulate others to get what they want. They lack empathy because it serves them no purpose to care about their negative effect on others. According to the Mayo Clinic, boasting and feeling superior to others around you isn't a sign of too much self-esteem. It's more likely evidence of insecurity and low self-worth. The view that some people are more important, and others are less important, creates a false view for oneself as well as everyone else.

These two viewpoints of low self-worth create an unhealthy imbalance between selfishness and selflessness that favors one while shortchanging another. Oddly, people pleasers and narcissists often attract each other to help substantiate each other's distorted self-view. They are both trying to feel better about themselves at the expense of themselves or others.

Low self-worth also is the premise for the foundation of discrimination. According to the *Cambridge Dictionary*, the word "discriminate" is a verb (a word that shows action or a state of being) that means *to see a difference, to treat a person or particular group of people differently and especially unfairly in a way that is worse than the way people are usually treated.*

People harboring negative self-beliefs need to identify, challenge and correct these beliefs in order to truly feel better about themselves and have a healthy self-worth. However, what often happens instead is that these people try to build themselves up by diminishing and holding back others. The less others achieve, the better these people look. They typically target people who are different than them in some way. This judgmental act makes them feel superior to others but doesn't actually make them superior human beings. They just think and feel like they are ... at least temporarily. It has nothing to do with the people they devalue and everything to do with their inner need to feel better about themselves. This works particularly well for them when others buy into and accept that they are inferior.

This is a poor attempt to fill an emptiness in a person's self-worth by using a false and splintered truth, but it never fills the void. There is an ever-present yearning from within that still remains. It's an inner voice that's loving and one that refuses to give up on us knowing the truth about ourselves, a single truth that applies to all. It's the discovery of who we are and the power we possess, and it's a shared journey that we are all on.

15. SEE YOUR ROLE

T o think that some or all of our actions do not have any effect or are without consequence is not logical. Our participation, effort and persistence — or lack of these — always create an effect of some kind. This is just how it is. If it's our experience, then we've contributed to creating it in some way. We can't be absent from the creation of our own results. The challenge lies in seeing what we are doing or not doing to create our outcomes and experiences — as well as seeing what we did or didn't do that contributed to bringing about our past results. Seeing our role becomes next to impossible, however, when we deny playing a role at all. It's a Catch-22. We can't see it so we deny it, and because we deny it, we can't see it.

There are infinite ways we play a role in creating our results, with some ways creating better results than others. Merely showing up is a way we play a role. Participating is playing a role, and so is continuing to participate. Putting up with and tolerating is playing a role, too. Giving up is playing a role. "I can" and "I can't" thinking play roles. Seeking a solution plays a role, and not seeking a solution plays a role. Hard work and persistence play roles, and so do their absence. With every decision we make or put off making, we're playing a role in what we create.

Shifting our perspective to see things we couldn't see before is the key to realizing our role. And seeing our role is the key to flying higher. It's like the jungle picture with the hidden tigers. I remember one titled "Can You Find the 16 Tigers?" The image has four tigers in plain sight, but most are hidden in foliage and trees. When you stare at it for long enough, the tigers begin appearing all over the place, but the last one or two are the hardest to find. For the life of me, I couldn't see that last one. I looked and looked and looked. Because I couldn't see it, I started to doubt whether it even existed. They must have made a mistake and left it out. It's the same with our perspective regarding the role we play in creating our results. We did the right thing, but the wrong thing happened, and we cannot see anything we did wrong that caused it. Therefore, there is no connection between our actions and our outcomes.

There is something that shifts in our perspective when we can finally see that last tiger. You couldn't see it … you couldn't see it

… you couldn't see it … and then it happens. You can see it! Now you can't stop seeing it. It happened in an instant and the only thing that changed was your perspective. That 16th tiger was always there. And the role you play in creating your results has always been there, too. Seeing it is what makes changing ourselves make sense.

Seeing the tigers in this analogy is about seeing what is there but is hidden from us. It's there whether we can see it or not. If we can't see the role we are playing, we disown our results and place blame elsewhere for causing it. And most importantly, we don't fix it. We become trapped with nothing of significance changing in our lives as long as we cannot see our role.

While we wait for our life to change, life is patiently waiting for us to change.

Keep looking for the tigers! Others can see them and so can we. This equally applies to organizations and accurately seeing the role they are playing in creating their results. An example of this is when employers fail to make the connection between disengaged employees and their decisions to hire. Rather than making their selection process better, they place their focus on trying to change their poor performing employees. The hiring missteps continue and nothing dramatically improves.

The next five chapters outline changes in attitude that can not only change your results and improve your life, but also lead you to the discovery of the great power you possess. Implementing these changes is how YOU become an Attitude Revolutionist.

16. DARE TO BELIEVE

The first change in attitude is to dare to believe when you don't. It sounds easy enough ... doesn't it? But how do you believe something is possible when you just can't fathom it? Let's break it down. Low performers commonly believe they can't achieve a goal because obstacles block their way. High performers have obstacles, too. Neither knows how to overcome their obstacles initially. This makes high performers and low performers in the same boat at the beginning.

Obstacles are particularly notable because they are the fork in the road where a person's attitude must decide which direction to go in — "I can" or "I can't" — all before the person knows how. This is a decision-making moment that has great outcome-determining impact for every human being. That's because everything else that follows is based on which road a person takes. You would think a

64

decision this important would take some time to determine. But it doesn't. It happens fast. Like blinking, we're often unaware we're doing it, but we are.

Becoming aware of our habit of responding to challenges is the first step in breaking the habit. "I can't" thinking isn't some celestial message that it's not meant to be. It's a way of thinking that was picked up and adopted in childhood when "I can" thinking wasn't learned. The way a child develops an "I can" attitude is the same way an adult develops it, too. It takes some obstacle-conquering successes to fully embrace this belief. That means we must step into some challenges we think we can't conquer in order to discover that we can.

Eleanor Roosevelt, wife of the 32nd U.S. president Franklin D. Roosevelt, once said: "You must do the things you think you cannot." She added, "You gain strength, courage and confidence by every experience in which you really stop to look fear in the face."

First, you must catch your predictions of a dire outcome and then start challenging them. They aren't some logical rationale with a lot of data analyzed that comes to a valid conclusion. They are a split-second judgment call based on how many obstacles we did or did not conquer in childhood. It's simple. If you conquered more challenges than you didn't in your youth, then you'll lean toward thinking you can as an adult. "I can't" isn't "I can't do it." It's more about "I'm too scared to try."

Next, deliberately negate your limited beliefs. You don't need to believe you can before you stop thinking that you can't. Reverse your thinking and slam it into neutral. Otherwise you'll start building an outcome that you really don't want. You must stop the momentum of "I can't" thinking, and no one can do this for you.

Start saying to yourself, "I can do this." Say it repeatedly. Align your thoughts with the outcome that you want to achieve rather than using your thoughts to work against you. It doesn't matter who you are, this is something we all need to practice. When we hit a wall or experience a setback, no matter the obstacle, we must play a mind game with ourselves. We must tell ourselves we can do it. We must fake THE ATTITUDE until our attitude makes it there. And it will. The more your unruly mind fills your head with doubt, wrestle it back. Take charge and keep changing your thinking. Do this over and over again. Your old ways will eventually give way. Only when you neutralize your negativity can thoughts of possibility begin to seep in.

There is a story about classical artist and sculptor Michelangelo, who was asked how he ever created the magnificent lifelike statue of David. If you've ever seen it up close, it looks real enough that it could just walk off its pedestal. Michelangelo responded by saying he had just chipped off the excess rock. When we chip away at our own limited thinking, what's underneath is magnificent. When this excess kryptonite-like rock is removed, just below the surface is the truth of what can be, and it's just waiting to be revealed to us.

17. RELENTLESSLY SEEK SOLUTIONS

I have some fundamental questions about where solutions come from. For example, why do they come to one person and not another? Are they readily available to all? Where do solutions come from when they pop into our mind? Do we already have them tucked away in our brain, and if yes, are the same solutions in everyone's brain? How do we come up with solutions to things that we've never done before, or no one has ever done — like getting a man on the moon in the 1960s?

What I know for sure is that people come up with some amazing ideas and ways to achieve their goals. Massachusetts Institute of Technology researchers invented a way to use a laser to shrink 3D objects to nanoscale, a size so small a microscope is required to see it. Several people found solutions for handling human waste in space, something that was necessary for longer space missions. It's as if there's a giant pool that's filled with creative ideas and solutions, and our job is to dive in and keep diving in until we come up with the one that produces the outcome we want.

Achievement involves knowing the rules, not ignoring them. In his 1994 book *I Can't Accept Not Trying: Michael Jordan on the Pursuit of Excellence*, professional basketball phenomenon Michael Jordan wrote the following:

If you're trying to achieve, there will be roadblocks. I've had them; everybody has had them. But obstacles don't have to stop you. If you run into a wall, don't turn around and give up. Figure out how to climb it, go through it, or work around it.

Great accomplishment has never been about achieving only when it's easy and obstacle-free. And neither has it ever been about having accomplishments freely handed to us without us first doing the necessary work. Vidal Sassoon, a British hairstylist who built an empire that today includes one of the world's most prominent product lines, is famous for the quote, "Only in the dictionary does success come before work." Success is not about "gimmes" or entitlement. The bottom line is those who fail to find a solution only find failure.

The fundamental difference between people who achieve goals and those who fall short is the latter too often fail to find a solution. They give up too soon, and as a result, never take flight. Giving up will always be the easiest path to take and an option for everyone no matter who you are. The process of achievement is an impersonal and straightforward process. If you don't find a way to overcome your obstacles, you don't get to the goal. Period. High performers simply find more solutions. As an Attitude Revolutionist, that's what you must do. So how do you do it? You add one very simple word to your "I don't know hows" and that word is "yet."

"I don't know how ... yet" points our thinking in the right direction and cranks up the problem-solving part of our brain. It lights it up and directs our brain cells to go find a solution. Sometimes we wake up in the middle of the night with the answer. The brain takes those orders and relentlessly begins searching for an answer whether we're consciously thinking about it or not.

It's even a good idea to start an Attitude Mastermind Group. Be selective in who you invite. You want to avoid whiners and complainers and only invite people whose opinions you trust and respect. The objective is to share advice and help each other come up with ideas and ways to solve problems. Two to 10 people work best and this can be done personally or at work.

Not all ideas we come up with will be viable solutions. We won't know which ones will work and which ones won't without giving them a try. Discovering a solution takes courage. It requires the willingness to try and fail. It's an ongoing process of try and fail and try and fail and try again. It's a test of grit, ingenuity and perseverance between you and the obstacles. The only one standing at the end wins. British billionaire, business magnate, author and philanthropist Richard Branson said: "My attitude has always been, if you fall flat on your face, at least you're moving forward. All you have to do is get back up and try again."

When chemicals are mixed together, such as baking soda and vinegar, a reaction occurs that's almost explosive. This reaction is neither right nor wrong, it's just the result of those two chemicals being combined. To get a different chemical reaction as an outcome — let's say a more bubbly, effervescent effect — you must figure the right chemicals to mix that will produce that result. Every mixture that creates the wrong outcome is a learning opportunity. It informs you what doesn't work to create the results you want. You cannot keep mixing the same chemicals and expect the chemicals to alter their normal reaction to fit your desires. And you can't just sit there wishing and hoping and praying for the outcome to just happen. You've got to do the work. Your job is to figure out the formula that will create those effervescent bubbles you want. This is the fundamental understanding that you always play a role in creating your results — meaning that in order to change your results, you must change what you do until you get the results you want.

Our second change in attitude is to make sure we are activating solution-oriented thinking every single time we encounter an obstacle. And when it comes to relentlessly seeking solutions, it's worth noting something spectacular that often happens in the process of achieving a goal. Sometimes random strangers cross our path and give us the answer we were seeking. Sometimes an unexpected door opens, and it becomes the solution to our problem. Sometimes something completely unrelated leads to another event that turns out to be exactly what we needed. If you pay close attention, you'll notice the power of the "I can" attitude activates something greater than us that orchestrates the bringing of solutions to us by means that have nothing to do with us. Our job is to have our eyes open to seeing them and our mind receptive to receiving them.

18. PROTECT YOUR ENERGY

O ur energy is very important, and that's why protecting it is attitude change number three. We need energy to go the distance to achieve goals. It's knowing the truth about our great power that gives us that energy. It's this energy that fuels us for the length of time it takes to get to a goal. It's the fuel behind self-motivation and is used to uncover solutions and conquer one obstacle after another. Without this fuel source, we're unable to bring our desires and goals to fruition. That means knowing about the power of attitude and using it intelligently is a key part of every success.

When people play the victim and place blame for their results elsewhere, they are denying their power. That disconnects them from this source of energy. It doesn't take much energy or effectiveness for an "I can't" attitude to prove something cannot be done. But that doesn't mean they don't want to achieve the goal. The contrary is often true. They want success just as much, if not more, than anyone else. It's their attitude that puts them at a huge disadvantage when it comes to attaining it.

What we focus on and give our attention to commands our energy. Healthy relationships give and receive energy freely, back and forth, by focusing on each other without a hidden agenda. In healthy relationships, people genuinely care about each other. When people perceive themselves to be powerless, they behave differently. They take in the energy of others without giving much in return. They receive energy, hold onto it, get more energy, hold onto it, take more energy from others and so on. To do this, they must get others to notice and pay attention to them. Some create conflict to get attention. Others pretend they're the victim in hopes of garnering sympathy and commiseration. Some use the attention of others to offload heavy drama … and then walk away. They feel better. The other person feels drained.

The worst energy-draining tactic is when people act superior, belittling and finding fault in others. They prey on other people who have low self-worth. That's because the more someone feels worthless or inferior, the easier that person is to control. These people who disparage others not only increase their own energy, they also decrease the energy of these other people, leaving others feeling depleted.

Whenever people spend their time complaining to others about something that's not working in their lives, but have little interest in changing or make no attempt to solve their problems, it's an irritation without action. It's a sign of a powerless mindset. And just listening to them can cause us to feel drained. No matter how much we think we can fix other people or their problems, our efforts won't solve the core issue. People often reject solutions or create new ones just to keep the attention of others to siphon more energy.

The best way to help people with a powerless perspective is to avoid enabling them. Don't give them your energy if they aren't going to use it wisely to move themselves forward. This book is all about helping people … who are willing to help themselves. It's not about endlessly expending energy with no return on investment. It's not our responsibility to solve others' problems. We do them no favors by taking away this responsibility of theirs and doing it for them. Doing so only slows their growth and keeps them from learning to slay their own dragons themselves. It's in learning how that we discover we *can* — which, in turn, changes our attitude in a way that makes us no longer dependent on other people for our source of energy. This is the key to helping others. Organizations would be wise to comprehend this. Rather than focusing on improving performance by finding better ways to engage the disengaged, they should hire people who have an effective attitude to start with.

People who have not yet tapped into the power of attitude need the energy of others to put them in motion, and as a result, will never achieve their full potential. Rather than giving them your energy, which does neither them nor an organization any favors, a better strategy is to point them in the direction of seeking a solution and let them take over. Here what you can say:

- *What are you going to do to resolve your problem?*
- *I'm confident you will figure out the right solution.*
- *I'm busy now and can't talk. I'm sure you can handle your situation.*

Your positive energy is an asset to you and others. That makes it a hot commodity worth protecting. Energy-dependent people will feed off anyone who is willing to give them time and attention. Become aware of those who make you feel drained or seem disinterested in finding solutions. Be cautious of those who disrespect and cross your boundaries. Those who are overly critical, are dramatic or are chronic complainers. And those who are unreliable, unsupportive or selfish. They're all signs of a relationship that is out to steal your energy. Become unwilling to give your attention to dead-end situations and chronically out-of-balance relationships. Sacrificing yourself doubles the number of those with inadequate energy to achieve their goals.

"To go against the dominant thinking of your friends, of most of the people you see every day, is perhaps the most difficult act of heroism you can have."

Theodore H. White
American political journalist and historian

When we want to maximize our energy, that's when we become more aware of the energy of the people around us. By surrounding ourselves with people who are willing to uplift and energize each other, to learn and grow, to give and receive, and to support one another, we can amplify our energy instead of depleting it. The extra boost of energy we get back from others becomes the wind under our wings that enables us to fly a little higher. The energy we give back to them does the same for them. It's mutually validating!

19. BECOME INTOLERANT

We generally think being tolerant is a good thing. It means we accept people who are unlike us. But being tolerant can be a bad thing, too. For example, tolerance is never a good thing when it comes to putting up with unacceptable or abusive behavior from others. Tolerating mediocrity isn't good. Tolerating someone who's lazy or unreliable is not good, either. And it's never acceptable for people to always talk just about themselves and show little interest in others. People get away with it all the time. It's when we keep tolerating behaviors that shortchange us that we play the role of enabler.

Reaching the point of enough and becoming intolerant is a powerful shift in thinking that makes it the fourth attitude change. This shift is not about others changing — it's about how we respond when they don't. When we continue tolerating what's not working for us, then we have resigned ourselves to "This is as good as it gets" thinking. This keeps us from moving through our challenges and arriving at a better place. It inhibits greater flight.

"People say, "That's just the way it is." I say "Things are only the way you let them be."

Lee Cockerell, retired executive vice president of Walt Disney World

---

Let's face it, authentic expression is not something that always comes easily. There's a delicate balance between saying what you mean and saying it with tact. It's often easier to say what another person wants to hear rather than speaking the truth. Fear of rejection, a negative judgment or a bad reaction can hinder some people from saying what needs to be said.

Maggie Kuhn, aging advocate and founder of the Gray Panthers activist group, said, "Stand before the people you fear and speak your mind — even if your voice shakes." Speaking up is how we communicate and establish our boundaries. However, it's our silence that sends the loudest message of all. It tells others what they can get away with.

People can react in numerous ways when hearing a difficult message. One person gets angry and argumentative, and another turns on the tears. Someone else becomes remorseful and motivated to change. How another person reacts is not up to you. Poor reactions are often used to intimidate, control and stifle communication. Children's book author Dr. Seuss said, "The best advice I ever heard: Be who you are and say what you feel because people who mind don't matter and people who matter don't mind." Our job is to speak up regardless of how a person reacts. But it's how a person reacts that tells us who matters most.

I remember a story told to me by a man who decided to start a moving business with a friend. He rented a truck, and before you knew it, jobs started coming in. The money was excellent. The friend, however, liked to party late into the night. You can imagine what happened next. He became unreliable. To make the business work, his partner knew he needed to surround himself with people he could count on. He took a bold move that later got a name — "Hot 30." As his friend called and inquired about the next job, he simply said he had it covered. In reality, he was nervous about how to handle large moving jobs involving appliances and big pieces of furniture without any assistance. But what happened next was unexpected and good.

At the same time that he decided not to tolerate to his friend's unacceptable behavior, all the moving jobs that came in for the next 30 days were small enough for him to handle himself. His friend eventually came around and realized the negative impact of his behavior on his friend, the business and himself. After being in what he called the "hot seat" for 30 days, he made a change. In the workplace it's called feedback and progressive discipline. Whether at work or personally, we must deal with it to rise above it. People aren't typically motivated to alter themselves when there's no consequence. It's when behavior isn't tolerated that the greatest chance for change exists. This is common sense for some, but not the case for all.

We must become good at standing up for ourselves and saying "no" and even better at maintaining strong and healthy boundaries. We trap ourselves by holding out for others to change, but we empower and free ourselves when we become the ones willing to do the changing. Ultimately, we are responsible for who we let into our lives, and our organizations, as well as who we allow to stay in.

As our attitude shifts, so will the people in our life. Some people will change while others won't. Putting distance between ourselves and those who won't is often the best thing to do. Jim Collins, best-selling author of *Good to Great*, said it well when he said get "the wrong people off the bus." Those who do change, however, do so because they were willing. Never take credit for the changes another person made or take responsibility for the ones people need to make.

Within each of us there is an inner urge to live our best life. It's a prodding that refuses to settle for less than what can be. Abraham Maslow, an American psychologist, described this as self-actualization or "What a man can be, he must be."

20. PURSUE YOUR PASSION

P assion is a self-motivation powerhouse. It motivates us to jump out of bed and to look forward to our day ahead. Time flies when we're doing something we love, and it drags when we're not. When you're passionate about what you do, it's obvious to others. American media executive, actress, talk show host, television producer and philanthropist Oprah Winfrey once said: "Passion is energy. Feel the power that comes from focusing on what excites you." That's why pursing it is change number five.

As an "I can't" attitude yields to optimism, there is one question that's always asked. "Since I have the power to create, what do I want to create?" The reply that follows is always a no-brainer. It's to answer our inner calling to do what we love. Passion guides us to be authentic with ourselves and to live the life we were meant to live.

83

We live our life by design, not by default. It's no coincidence that our passion aligns with our talents, our gifts, and our circumstances, too. Our passion steers us in a specific direction, one that's right for us. Passion doesn't just serve us — it serves others, too. When we follow our passion, our contribution makes the world a little better place than it was before. It's like being a piece of a big puzzle that no one else can fill.

"Destiny is not a matter of chance; it is a matter of choice. It is not something to be waited for, but rather something to be achieved."

William Jennings Bryan

When we comprehend the power of attitude, we naturally gravitate away from what we don't like and what doesn't work for us and move toward what does. But following our passion doesn't mean doing only those things we like to do and skipping the rest. Most jobs, even the ones we love, include a combination of tasks we like and dislike. It's our willingness to do whatever it takes, including those tasks we don't like — and do them well — that enables us to move forward and achieve goals. It's doing the hard work now that increases our likelihood of a good payoff later.

Many successful CEOs started at the bottom and worked their way up. They began in entry-level jobs they didn't necessarily love. Imagine if they had avoided doing the parts they didn't like? They would never have moved up and been given more responsibility. We often don't like tasks that we find challenging. Conquering challenges is typically not at the top of anyone's list of favorite things to do. Sidestepping them may make our life easier today, but doing the hard work to overcome them still remains ahead.

Passion is like a sticky glue that keeps us in the game, especially when we don't like doing a task. Passion helps us to discover what we really can do by keeping us from giving up, and it draws us back in when we do. It gives us the courage and staying power to conquer our challenges. Passion helps us to discover an "I can" attitude, and an "I can" attitude helps us to fulfill our passion. When an "I can" attitude (the power of mind) joins forces with what the heart loves (the power of passion), that's when the greatest results occur. Together, they can move mountains and land on a moon.

21. AIN'T IT THE TRUTH

I n the 1939 movie classic *The Wizard of Oz*, the young girl Dorothy, who lives on a farm in Kansas, is bumped on the head during a tornado, touching off her adventure into the Land of Oz. She meets a scarecrow who wishes he had a brain, a tin man who would love a heart, and a cowardly lion who more than anything wants courage. The entire story is about the obstacles Dorothy and her newfound friends face on their journey to find the Great Wizard of Oz, the only one who can fulfill their desires.

Toward the end of the film, when the Wizard is granting them their wishes, he says to the Cowardly Lion: "As for you, my fine friend, you are a victim of disorganized thinking. You are under the delusion that simply because you run away from danger, you have no courage. You are confusing courage with wisdom!" When he receives his medal of honor engraved with the word "Courage," the Lion replies, "Ain't it the truth! Ain't it the truth!" The only thing that changed when the Lion transformed from cowardly to courageous was his thinking and really nothing else. This change of thinking happened in an instant.

But that isn't the most profound part of the movie, and neither is the fact that Dorothy and her friends overcome all the obstacles they encounter along the way no matter how big, bad and scary they appear to be. I believe the best part is when the Wizard is about to leave the Land of Oz to take Dorothy back home to Kansas. Just when his hot air balloon is lifting up, Dorothy's beloved dog, Toto, jumps from her arms. She can't leave without him, so she leaps out of the balloon's basket to retrieve him and it launches without her.

Almost out of the blue, Glenda the Good Witch of the North appears. Dorothy begs for her help to get back to Kansas. The beautiful witch responds, "You don't need to be helped any longer. You've always had the power." Confused, Dorothy responds, "I have?" Even the Scarecrow jumps in and asks, "Then why didn't you tell her before?"

Here is the part that is so hard to believe was written almost a century ago. The Good Witch answers, "Because she wouldn't have believed me. She had to learn it for herself!" Dorothy is asked what she has learned and responds, "Well, I think that it wasn't enough to just want to see Uncle Henry and Auntie Em." And it's not enough for us just to have dreams or just to want to reach a goal. The Scarecrow with his brain says, "But it's so easy, I should have thought of it for you, Dorothy." "No," the Good Witch says, "She had to find it out for herself."

Many people still have not learned how to use the power of attitude effectively simply because they don't believe they have this power. That's why they look outside of themselves for an external wizard, someone or something more powerful than themselves, to grant them their dreams and goals by removing for them the obstacles that block their path. And it's all because they don't believe they can do it for themselves. If you haven't seen *The Wizard of Oz* lately, it's a lot of fun to watch it for its deeper message. The moral of the story is it's all about discovering for ourselves our own power to produce desired outcomes.

22. PATIENTLY WAITING

T here is nothing magical here — no fairly dust to sprinkle or spell to cast that will work in the absence of the effort and commitment to form more effective thinking habits. No one can do this for you, and you can't do it for anyone else. It is strictly a do-it-yourself process. There are no shortcuts, either. Before you begin, let me tell you that forming a new thinking habit will be easier when everything is good and going smoothly. The greatest challenge in changing your way of thinking will exist when your life isn't going so well. But that's also the time when tapping into the power of attitude becomes the most important.

There is a good chance that when you begin switching your well-entrenched thinking that has had operating authority for most of your life, you will have contradictory thoughts such as, "Are you nuts? There's no way I can do that!" That's OK. This is normal, especially in the beginning.

Starting a new habit doesn't mean the first time you try it, it's going to instantly take hold. It won't. The old habit must give up some ground to make room for your new way of thinking to take root. This is how it works. The more you reframe your thinking, the more it will become a conditioned habit.

Essentially, you will be unthinking "I can't" and then rethinking "I can." The very first thing you must do is boot out your limited thinking. Keeping it will only constrict your mental effectiveness and productivity. Next, switch your thinking to conceiving the desired outcome as being possible. You are changing "There is no way!" to "How can I?" Then redirect your thoughts to figuring out what it will take to produce the desired outcome. The latter expands your mind and directs it to go find a solution. Remember, it's your thinking — therefore, it's your choice. You're in charge! While you're transitioning your own attitude, who you surround yourself with is of critical importance. It's a vulnerable time for you. I highly recommend getting an Attitude Mentor and even wearing an Attitude Revolutionist wristband as a reminder to stay strong.

Here's a retraining technique that helped me. All it requires is you and a rubber band. It will help speed up forming a new habit if you're really committed. Simply place the rubber band on your wrist and every time — yes, I mean every time — you catch yourself thinking or saying "I can't" or any variation, snap it. No more than a little pop is needed. It's not supposed to be negative torture treatment, just a friendly retraining reminder to unthink what you just thought and rethink something better. Something like, "Ok ... it's possible. I just need to figure out how!" Any variation of "How can I?" that will turn on the problem-solving part of your brain will be satisfactory.

In essence, what you are doing is getting your yeses and nos straight. They are reversed when you think "I can't" thoughts. "I can't" works to keep us from getting to our goals. We're creating what we don't want instead of creating what we do want. That's definitely backwards!

Now it's time to say "yes" to what we want. I remember an event in my life that taught me this lesson. I had always wanted to go to the Grand Canyon and see its magnificence for myself, but I had never done it. I was speaking in Phoenix, Arizona, about a three-hour drive from the canyon, and I kept saying to myself, "Why don't you just go and do it?" I kept coming up with a bunch of reasons why I couldn't or shouldn't. I thought to myself, "I don't have the time. I'd have to change my airline ticket. I didn't pack for a trip to the Grand Canyon. I don't have a rental car. I have no hotel room booked there. I don't want to go by myself." Shall I go on, or do you get my point?

At some point I gave myself permission to say "Yes!" instead of "No!" Suddenly, my thinking aligned with my desires. When I switched my thinking from all the reasons why I couldn't do it to focusing on how I could pull it off, everything seemed to change in that instant — no joke. I made a call to the airline to see whether there was a seat open on the same flight on the following day, and there was. I called my travel agent and discovered a car was available for rent just a few blocks away from where I was speaking.

Once I said "Yes!" everything happened so easily, I kid you not. I got a ride to the rental car, got directions and was quickly on my way. When I arrived, I started talking with people in a tour group at the Grand Canyon and they invited me to join them for dinner. I said "Yes, thank you." I ate rattlesnake, which was quite a new experience. Even though I was unprepared for a 50-degree temperature drop that evening, I was generously loaned a sweater to keep me warm. It didn't stop there. I found a beautiful hotel that had room for me, and I saw the most magnificent sunset and sunrise overlooking the Grand Canyon.

My 24-hour extended trip to the Grand Canyon could not have been any more fabulous. And to think, I could have missed this amazing experience simply by focusing my thoughts on all the reasons why I couldn't go. It made me wonder how many other things I had I missed out on. When I looked back at all those reasons that I had told myself regarding why I couldn't go, I wondered whose side I had been on. I realized how my own thinking was working against me and holding me back, and that all I needed to say was, "Yes I can" … and start saying it a whole lot more!

That trip to the Grand Canyon also taught me that you don't need to have all the answers on how to pull something off first, that you can still say "yes" and then figure out how to do it as you go. In fact, that's exactly how high achievers operate. They don't have all the answers before they're willing to believe they can. It's not that we have to say yes to everything. But sometimes we say we can't … when we really can do it.

This quote from author, poet and philosopher Eden Phillpotts sums up my experience best, "The universe is full of magical things and it's patiently waiting for our wits to grow sharper."

23. THE ATTITUDE REVOLUTION

Your attitude matters. But so does the attitude of those around you both personally and professionally. That's because attitude is contagious. Other people's attitude will have an effect on your own attitude. The energy of attitude flows from one person to another. Our energy flows to whatever or whoever we give our attention to, and it flows to us from those who give attention to us. The energy that is flowing isn't always good energy, however. Pay attention to whether your energy level increases or decreases when you're around someone. That's life's way of telling you who you should stay around or avoid. No one — I mean *no one* — gets a free pass to treat us poorly or negatively affect our energy.

Pessimism — a "Life is against me" attitude — is not benign. It drains us. This perspective of powerlessness goes into the ears of those listening and brings them down. It's an attempt to kill the optimism and great potential of others, short-circuit their momentum and hinder their flight. When we give our time and attention to any form of the belief in powerlessness, we are spending our precious energy — energy that could be better spent elsewhere — to prop up the dysfunctional attitude of another. Sadly, the people to need to hear this message the most are often the ones who want to hear it the least.

When others drop their problems on us without participating in finding solutions, they make our load heavier. When they complain, blame and put others down, they whittle away at our own belief in the power to create. When they disparage our dreams and goals, they weaken our attitude still more. It's our job to protect our positive sense of power and the energy it generates. It takes courage to speak up and say "Stop."

When we are silent, it hurts us the most. However, our silence also hurts others, including those who are willing to change and those who are not. We must keep healthy boundaries to protect our attitude from those who are not willing to change. A word of caution regarding your own perspective here: If someone else's objectionable behavior continues, don't blame that person. It's not that person doing something to us, but rather it is us doing something to ourselves. It's our continued participation, our mere presence, that is playing a role in shortchanging ourselves and our results. If only we could get them to change then we would not have to do the uncomfortable task of changing ourselves. When no one changes, nothing changes.

It's only when we become unwilling to tolerate that we become the one willing to change. We change by becoming intolerant to what we once accepted. We change by speaking up and saying "ENOUGH!!!" Being pushed to our limits moves us through our greatest transformation. That includes an organization's transformation, too. Bless the lessons, for they are good even though they often feel so bad. We are repeatedly given opportunities to discover our power to create, opportunities that are brilliantly camouflaged as impossible situations, insurmountable challenges and problematic people. It's the attitude we choose right here, in the face of a challenge, that determines whether we learn the lesson or get to repeat it.

It's against the wind that airplanes take off, kites fly higher and trees grow stronger. When it comes to achievement, many people miss the fact that it's a process of overcoming obstacles. We must climb the mountain to reach the peak. It's an uphill process and one that lifts us higher along the way. It's a journey that always involves obstacles. So, what's all the confusion? Why do people give up so easily and insist it's just not meant to be? I am amazed that in the 21st century there are still so many who don't comprehend the basic principles of achievement. Achievement is fundamentally about one thing — realizing that we can rise above our challenges and achieve our goals. In doing so, what we think we can do rises. It's not so much about what we accomplish, but rather, it's about who we become as a result of going through this process.

Mankind has such great potential. Mildred Norman, also known as the "Peace Pilgrim," said, "If you realized how powerful your thoughts are, you would never think a negative thought." She believed humanity has only scratched the surface of its real potential. I believe she's right.

So much potential is unwittingly wasted on ineffective thinking. It's incalculable the loss of human potential caused by an "I can't" attitude. Even the loss of your own. And no doubt, there is a monumental loss of organizational potential as well. That's because we don't just hire people's skill sets, we hire their attitude, too. That attitude will affect what people will achieve, and it will impact their coworkers, too. It will become woven into the very fabric of the corporate culture. The wrong attitude will create a caustic and negative environment, and as long as it's kept, that organization will never achieve maximum success.

Organizations need a better strategy for success than motivating the unmotivated (using one person to light a fire under others to get them to do their job). Employee engagement tactics actually backfire by inadvertently validating the mindset of the unmotivated, those who believe the power to produce results doesn't reside within. Organizations have a great opportunity, even an obligation, to play an impactful role by helping their employees' discovery of the truth about their power to achieve, rather than hindering it by enabling and reinforcing the false notion of powerlessness and external control.

What we are willing to put up with as individuals and in the workplace is an indicator of the level of development, or underdevelopment, of our own attitude. The bottom line is we only have as much of THE ATTITUDE as we are willing to demonstrate.

The reality is ... we are in serious need of an attitude change. We need a 21st century worldwide *Attitude Revolution*, like the Industrial and Agriculture Revolutions ... *but for the mind.* In the 18th and early 19th centuries, the Industrial Revolution had a profound effect as it spread throughout the world and changed life for the better. Unlike any other time in history, inventions came at a rapid speed — inventions such as the light bulb, the sewing machine, radio, television, airplanes and so much more, none of which had existed prior. The Agricultural Revolution marked a period of new farming techniques and improvements that resulted in increased crop production. Better crop yields paved the way for feeding more livestock and ultimately led to people being better-nourished and healthier.

A *revolution* marks a period of sudden shift in humanity. It's an era of accelerated change that leads to a dramatic transformation for the better. It's a mass shift, and in this case a shift in thinking, that happens one person at a time, *starting with you*, but with a lot of others doing it, too — including entire organizations. It's this Attitude Revolution that reinvents our understanding of achievement and spawns a new model. This new model makes it trendy to face our challenges and unacceptable to say "I can't." It makes it normal to acknowledge our failures, learn from them and persevere and abnormal to accept the excuses that powerless minds conjure up. In this new model, we take ownership for our results, whether they are good, bad or ugly. It becomes commonplace to have a mentor and uncommon to vent our problems without seeking a solution.

Imagine for a moment what can be.

Imagine the profound impact a mass shift in attitude, an Attitude Revolution, can have. Imagine a workplace adopting this mindset and all of its employees thinking "I can" thoughts. Imagine what could be accomplished. Imagine the problems that can be solved. Imagine the things we can invent, the suffering we can end, and the happiness that comes from living to our full potential and fulfilling our passion. This is possible! Just imagine what it will be like when more people become Attitude Revolutionists and *Have The Attitude* that makes great things happen! But best of all, as an Attitude Revolutionist yourself, imagine the profound difference you can make with the rise of your own attitude. Imagine looking at obstacles that you thought were insurmountable with an "I can" attitude. Imagine the excitement you feel. Imagine solutions to your problems popping into your mind. Imagine creative ideas and inspiration flowing to you, and imagine acting on them and bringing them to life when you are experiencing THE ATTITUDE for yourself!

It's as if life is one big schoolhouse purposefully designed to use challenges to wake us up to the truth of the great power we possess. Let the Attitude Revolution begin!

WWW.CAROLQUINN.COM

FOR THE ORGANIZATION

KEYNOTE SPEAKER: CAROL QUINN

Book a Keynote Presentation to start an Attitude Revolution in your organization or at your next event.

R enowned business author, CEO of Hire Authority, Inc., and keynote speaker Carol Quinn is the leading expert in understanding the common thread that all high performers share — THE ATTITUDE! In her best-selling book, *Motivation-Based Interviewing: A Revolutionary Approach to Hiring the Best*, Quinn helps employers improve their hiring by teaching them how they could better identify the true high achievers from those pretending to be. Her cutting-edge methodology involving motivation-based interviewing, MBI, was derived from her experience in interviewing thousands of job candidates in Corporate America.

In this book, she puts her knowledge and easy-to-read style to work on a more personal level, moving from how to hire the attitude to how to *Have The Attitude!* Invite Carol to your next corporate event or conference to WOW your audience with her popular keynotes.

Invite Carol to your next corporate event or conference to WOW your audience with her popular keynotes.

There's Only One Thing Better Than Reading the Book…
It's Experiencing THE ATTITUDE For Yourself!

SPEAKER INFORMATION:

Call: 561-231-0313, extension 700
Visit: www.CarolQuinn.com
Twitter: @CQAttitude
LinkedIn: Carol Quinn

LEARN HOW TO HIRE THE ATTITUDE
Motivation-Based Interviewing

H iring the best requires more than just assessing a candidate's skill. Interviewers must also determine the candidate's attitude toward overcoming obstacles and how passionate they are about achieving your goals — both proven predictors of future success. Motivation-based interviewing (MBI) takes no extra interviewing time and can be used to fill every job opening. There are many ways to learn MBI. You can read a book, take an online or an instructor-led course and even become a Certified MBI Trainer. To learn more visit www.HireAuthority.com.

All books available on Amazon.com

ATTITUDE REVOLUTIONIST WRISTBANDS
#AttitudeRevolutionist

T hese attractive ½" wristbands come in multiple colors. "ATTITUDE REVOLUTIONIST" appears on the outside and the inner text reads: "I revolt against the status quo attitude & I'm willing to do something about it!" It's a powerful affirmation to support and strengthen your attitude.

Augment your own Attitude Revolution and help promote organizational awareness of the power of attitude! To purchase these wristbands and other Have The Attitude merchandise go to:

www.HaveTheAttitude.com

ATTITUDE NOTES

ATTITUDE NOTES

ATTITUDE NOTES

ATTITUDE NOTES

Made in the USA
Columbia, SC
13 May 2019